Grief
is a
Mess

Written and Illustrated by Jackie Schuld

Copyright © 2015 Jackie Schuld All rights reserved.
Cover and Illustration Copyright © 2015 Jackie Schuld All rights reserved.

ISBN 10: 151875287X ISBN 13: 978-1518752872

For My Mum

I still cannot believe I have to live the rest of my life without you.

Thank you for loving me unconditionally, showing me how to laugh amidst pain, and encouraging me to use my skills to help others.

I love you more.

Grief is a mess

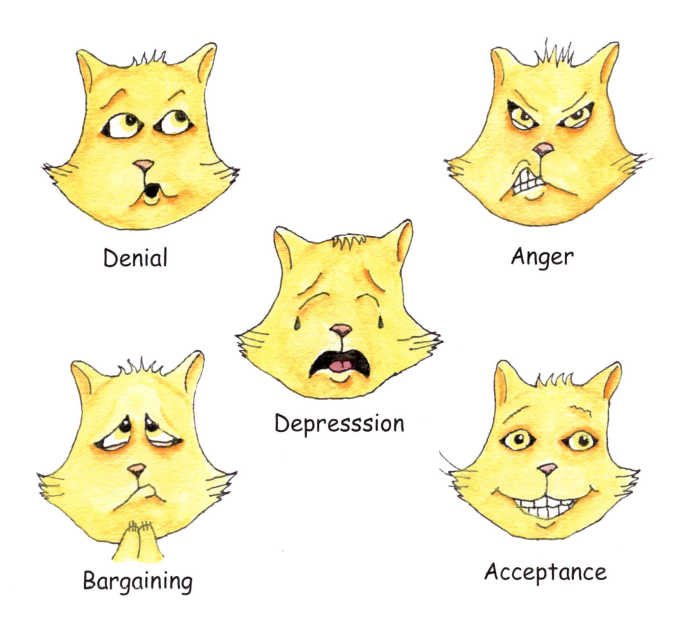

Someone tried to tidy it up with five stages

But grief isn't that simple

Because grief is different for everyone

Loneliness

Numbness

There are many emotions...

Fear

Rage

... that can be experienced

As well as...

10

Sleeplessness

Sickness

...physical effects

There are varying thoughts...

... about the loss

Staying Busy

Spiritual Practice

Because everyone experiences grief differently...

We all take different amounts of time to heal

It can be frustrating when others don't know how to help

However, their experience with grief may be different

Many want to help, but don't know how

It can be difficult to express what we need

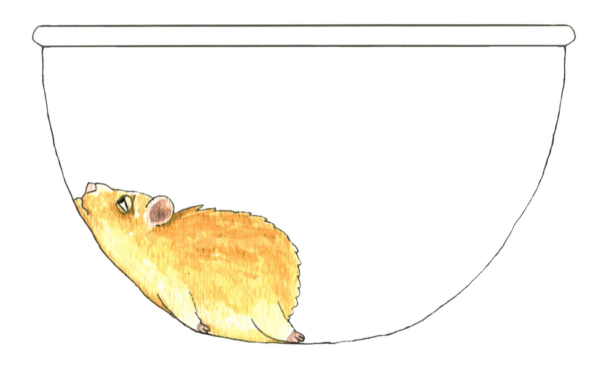

Especially when we may not know
how to overcome such pain

Gratefulness

New Appreciation for Life

Although there is nothing that can substitute for loss...

Empathy

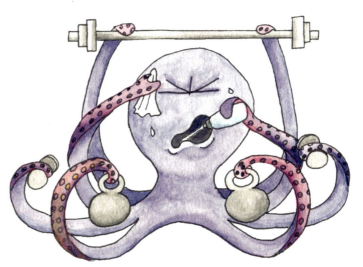

Motivation to Change

... there are positive things we can gain through grief

We can also rely on treasured memories...

...and the influence the person had on our lives

There are even moments we feel like ourselves again...

... and return to the things we love

But when a trigger causes pain to return...

... remember healing takes time

So be kind to yourself...

... and to others

Because we're all just trying to figure this mess out

About the Author

Jackie Schuld became a full-time artist after her mum passed away from Ovarian cancer in 2014. She currently lives in Tucson, AZ, where she can be found painting in her studio, teaching painting classes, shopping at thrift stores with her sister, discussing future projects with her brother, or enjoying nature with those she loves. She is grateful for the love and support her family and friends provide as she begins her career in art.

Resources

For "Grief is a Mess" discussion guides and art activities see www.jackieschuld.com

Jackie Schuld is available for speaking engagements and interactive classes addressing grief through art. If you would like to collaborate on a future project with her, she is interested in addressing psychological issues through art.

Jackie can be reached at jackieschuldart@gmail.com

Made in United States
Troutdale, OR
03/10/2024